1000 Years of Memories

The Remarkable LIFE STORIES of
TEN Individuals Who Have Reached
Age 100 and Beyond

TABLE OF CONTENTS

Dedication

(1907 – 2013)

This book is dedicated to the memory of my mother, Fannie S. Cohen, who was born on August 19, 1907 and passed away peacefully on January 5, 2013. From family to friends all who knew her were touched by an individual who had a loving and caring attitude. Throughout her 105+ years she exemplified the words "class" and "beauty". Her good deeds will be remembered by all who knew her.

Acknowledgements

Special thanks to my editor, Jim Lifter, whose hard work and creativity bought this book to life. Without his patience, diligence and fertile mind this project would have never been completed.

My heartfelt thanks to Keith Luscher for his work on the book cover and the overall assistance he has provided to this endeavor.

I also want to thank Rita Cohen, Genevieve Faehnle, and Bette Young who reviewed the material and provided their valuable insights and expertise. Their input was invaluable!

A big thank you to Lowell Mackenzie, Libby Patrick, Fran Rothman, Donna Merkle, Diana Bloch, Doug Weakley, Bette Young, and Ginny English for their referrals. They introduced me to some fabulous individuals.

Author Contact Information:

Website: www.1000yearsofmemories.com

e-Mail: DCohen1935@gmail.com

Phone: (614) 861-0778

Prologue

The first sad event that affected me was the death of my grandmother, Sarah Schilling in 1945--I was 10 years old. Unfortunately, as the years have passed, I have attended too many funerals. My mother, at age 106, passed away in 2013. I wish I had taken more time speaking with her about her dreams, successes, struggles and family history. I had the opportunity but never got around to it. My loss, my children's loss and my grandchildren's loss!!!!!

Everyone has a story and each story can enrich our lives.

With that in mind, you are going to read the stories of individuals who have reached the magic age of one hundred or beyond. One of the first questions I asked each person I interviewed was, "what is the earliest thing you remember?" Think about it – –**"what is the first thing you remember?"** If you are 20 years old, you may remember the dedication of the World War II Memorial in Washington D.C. If you are 40 you may recall the launch of STS-1 Columbia Space Craft. If you are 60 to 65 your first remembrances might be the assassination of President Kennedy, the Vietnam War or perhaps the Beatles. If you are 80, you certainly may remember Pearl Harbor and World War II. And if you are 90, the great depression of the 1930's is something that you could never forget.

To jog your memory, take a look at the following list of some significant events highlighting the last 100 years.

OCTOBER 8, 1918 – World War One: In the Argonne Forest in France, United States Cpl. Alvin C. York almost single handedly kills 25 German soldiers and captures 132.

AUGUST 11, 1919 – The Green Bay Packers are founded by Curly Lambeau.

AUGUST 18, 1920 –The 19th amendment gives women the right to vote.

JULY 29, 1921 – Adolf Hitler becomes Fuhrer of the Nazi party.

JULY 24, 1922 – Christian K. Nelson patents the Eskimo pie.

APRIL 18, 1923 – Yankee Stadium opens its doors in the Bronx, New York.

JANUARY 21, 1924 – Vladimir Lenin dies in Russia.

APRIL 10, 1925 – F. Scott Fitzgerald authors "The Great Gatsby."

AUGUST 23, 1926 – The sudden death of popular Hollywood actor Rudolph Valentino at the age of 31 causes mass grief and hysteria around the world.

JUNE 13, 1927 – A ticker – tape parade is held for aviator Charles Lindbergh down Fifth Avenue in New York City.

JUNE 28, 1928 – At the Democratic National Convention in Houston, New York Governor, Alfred E. Smith, becomes the first Catholic nominated by a major political party for president of the United States.

OCTOBER 24, 1929 – Wall Street crash: Three multi—digit percentage drops wipes out more than 30 billion dollars from the New York stock exchange (10 times greater than the annual budget of the Federal Government).

MARCH 12, 1930 – Mahatma Gandhi sets off on a 200-mile protest march towards the sea with 78 followers to protest the British monopoly on salt. More will join them during the salt March that ends on April 5.

MARCH 3, 1931 – The Star-Spangled Banner is adopted as the United States National Anthem.

MAY 2, 1932 – Comedian Jack Benny's radio show airs for the first time.

MARCH 4, 1933 – United States President Herbert Hoover is succeeded by Franklin D. Roosevelt who, in reference to the great depression proclaims, "the only thing we have to fear is fear itself" In his inauguration speech.

AUGUST 13, 1934 – The comic strip "Lil Abner" is first published in US newspapers.

JUNE 12, 1935 – Senator Huey Long of Louisiana makes the longest speech on Senate record, taking 15 ½ hours, and containing 150,000 words.

MARCH 1, 1936 – Construction of Hoover Dam is completed.

JULY 2, 1937 – A guard takes his place at the Tomb of the Unknowns in Washington, DC: continuous guards have been maintained there ever since.

JUNE 22, 1938 – Heavyweight boxer Joe Louis knocks out Max Schmelling in the first round of their rematch at Yankee Stadium in New York City.

FEBRUARY 8, 1939 – "Gone with the Wind" wins best picture at the Academy Awards.

APRIL 7, 1940 – Booker T. Washington becomes the first African-American to be depicted on a United States postage stamp.

DECEMBER 7, 1941 –The Japanese Navy launches a surprise attack on the United States fleet at Pearl Harbor, thus drawing the United States into World War II.

APRIL 9, 1942 – The Bataan peninsula falls, and the Bataan death march began.

JANUARY 15, 1943 – The Japanese are driven off Guadalcanal.

JUNE 6, 1944 –Battle of Normandy: Operation Overlord commonly known as D-Day.

AUGUST 10, 1945 – World War II: Japanese offers to surrender to the Allies.

JANUARY 10, 1946 – The first meeting of United Nations is held in London.

APRIL 1, 1947 – Jackie Robinson, the first African-American in modern major league baseball, signs a contract with the Brooklyn Dodgers.

APRIL 3, 1948 – President Harry S. Truman signs the Marshall Plan, which authorizes five million dollars in aid for 16 countries. It was the beginning of the Germany airlift.

JUNE 24, 1949 – First television Western, "Hopalong Cassidy", airs on NBC.

JANUARY 17, 1950 – Great Brinks robbery: 11 thieves steal more than two million dollars from an armored car in Boston, Massachusetts.

FEBRUARY 27, 1951 – The Twenty– second amendment to the United States Constitution, limiting presidents to two terms, is ratified.

JANUARY 14, 1952 – "Today" premieres on NBC, becoming one of the longest running television series in America.

JUNE 30, 1953 – The first Chevrolet Corvette is built at Flint, Michigan.

JANUARY 14, 1954 – Marilyn Monroe marries baseball player Joe DiMaggio.

SEPTEMBER 30, 1955 – Actor James Dean is killed when his automobile collides with another car in Chalaine, California.

APRIL 27, 1956 – Heavyweight boxing champion Rocky Marciano retires without losing a professional boxing match.

SEPTEMBER 26, 1957 –"West Side Story" has its first appearance on Broadway and runs for 732 performances.

JULY 7, 1958 – President Dwight D. Eisenhower signs the Alaska Statehood Act into US law.

FEBRUARY 16, 1959 – Fidel Castro becomes premier of Cuba.

SEPTEMBER 5, 1960 – 1960's summer Olympic Games: Cassius Clay wins the gold medal in light heavyweight boxing.

MAY 5, 1961 – Alan Shephard becomes the first American in space aboard Mercury – Redstone three.

MAY 31, 1962 – Nazi Adolf Eichmann is hanged at a prison in Israel.

NOVEMBER 22, 1963 – President Kennedy is assassinated in Dallas, Texas: VP Lyndon Baines Johnson becomes the 36th president of the United States.

JANUARY 18, 1964 – Plans to build the New York Trade Center are announced.

MARCH 2, 1965-"The Sound of Music" premieres at the Rivoli Theater in New York City.

MARCH 12, 1966 – Bobby Hull of the Chicago Blackhawks sets the National Hockey League single scoring record against the New York Rangers, with his 51st goal.

OCTOBER 26, 1967 – United States Navy pilot John McCain is shot down over North Vietnam and made a POW.

APRIL 4, 1968 – Civil rights leader Martin Luther King, Jr., 39, was shot and killed while standing on the balcony of the Lorraine Motel in Memphis, Tennessee.

JULY 20, 1969 – The lunar module Eagle lands on the lunar surface. An estimated five hundred million people world- wide watch in awe as Neil Armstrong takes his first steps on the moon.

APRIL 10, 1970 – Paul McCartney announces that the Beatles have disbanded.

FEBRUARY 8, 1971 – A new stock market index called the NASDAQ debuts. It was created by Bernie Madoff.

JANUARY 16, 1972 – Sugar bowl VI: the Dallas Cowboys defeat the Miami Dolphins 24 – 3.

JANUARY 27, 1973 – United States involvement in the Vietnam War ends with the signing of the Paris Peace Accords.

AUGUST 9, 1974 – Vice President Gerald Rudolph Ford succeeds Richard Milhouse Nixon as the 38th president of the United States.

MARCH 9, 1975 – Construction of the trans-Alaska pipeline system begins.

APRIL 1, 1976 – Apple Computer Company is formed by Steve Jobs and Steve Wozniak.

JUNE 26, 1977 – Elvis Presley performs his last ever concert at Market Square Arena in Indianapolis.

JUNE 12, 1978 – Serial killer David Berkowitz, the "Son of Sam," is sentenced to 365 years in prison.

MARCH 26, 1979 – In a ceremony at the White House, President Anwar Sadat of Egypt and Prime Minister Menachem Begin of Israel sign a peace treaty.

MAY 18, 1980 – Mount St. Helen erupts in Washington, killing 57 and causing The United States three billion dollars in damages.

JANUARY 20, 1981 – Iran releases 52 Americans held for 444 days within minutes of Ronald Reagan succeeding Jimmy Carter as the President of the United States.

JANUARY 13, 1982 – Shortly after takeoff, Air Florida flight 90 crashes into the Washington, DC's 14th St. Bridge and falls into the Potomac River, killing 78.

MARCH 23, 1983 – Strategic Defense Initiative: United States President Ronald Reagan makes his initial proposal to develop technology to intercept enemy missiles. The media dubbed this plan "Star Wars".

DECEMBER 3, 1984 – A leak from a Union Carbide plant in Bhopal, India kills 8000 people outright and injures over half a million in the worst industrial disaster in history.

OCTOBER 18, 1985--The Nintendo entertainment system, including the super Mario Brothers pack – man game is released.

APRIL 26, 1986 – The Chernobyl disaster: 4056 people killed and seven billion dollars of property damage.

JANUARY 8, 1987 – The Dow Jones industrial average closes above 2,000 for the first time in history.

APRIL 12, 1988 – Former pop singer Sonny Bono is elected mayor of Palm Springs, California.

JANUARY 24, 1989 – Serial killer Ted Bundy is executed in Florida's electric chair.

FEBRUARY 11, 1990 – Nelson Mandela is released from Verster Prison, near Cape Town, South Africa, after twenty-seven years behind bars.

JANUARY 16, 1991 – Gulf War: Operation Desert Storm begins with airstrikes against Iraq.

NOVEMBER 3, 1992 – Bill Clinton is elected 42nd president of the United States.

APRIL 19, 1993 – David Koresh is killed in the fire at the Branch Davidian compound near Waco, Texas.

MARCH 15, 1994 – United States troops are withdrawn from Somalia.

APRIL 19, 1995 – Oklahoma City bombings: 168 people, including eight federal marshals and 19 children are killed at the Alfred P. Murrah Federal Building.

MAY 11, 1996 – Florida to Atlanta bound ValuJet crashes in the Florida Everglades, killing all 110 on board.

AUGUST 1, 1997 – Steve Jobs returns to Apple Computer.

AUGUST 7, 1998 – Embassy bombings in Tanzania and Kenya kill 224 people and injure over 4500: they are linked to terrorist Osama Bin Laden.

JANUARY 1, 1999 – The Euro is established.

NOVEMBER 2, 2000 – The first resident crew enters the international space station.

SEPTEMBER 11, 2001 – Terrorists destroy the World Trade Center in New York City.

MARCH 12, 2002 – Andrea Yates is found guilty of drowning her five children.

OCTOBER 24, 2003 – The Concorde makes its last commercial flight.

APRIL 29, 2004 – The last Oldsmobile rolls off the assembly line.

APRIL 19, 2005 – Pope Benedict the 16th succeeds Pope John Paul the Second.

NOVEMBER 5, 2006 – Former President of Iraq, Saddam Hussein is sentenced to death by hanging by the special Iraqi special Tribunal.

JUNE 5, 2007 – NASA's messenger spacecraft makes its second flyby of Venus in route to Mercury.

FEBRUARY 19, 2008 – Fidel Castro announces his resignation as president of Cuba.

JUNE 25, 2009 – The death of American entertainer Michael Jackson triggers an outpouring of worldwide grief.

NOVEMBER 28, 2010 – Wiki-leaks releases a collection of more than 202,000 American diplomatic cables.

MAY 30, 2011 – Jim Tressel resigns as football coach at The Ohio State University.

NOVEMBER 6, 2012- President Barack Obama wins reelection by defeating Republican Mitt Romney.

MARCH 13, 2013- Pope Francis of Argentina is elected as the first Pope from the Americas.

NOVEMBER 10, 2014-The Republican Party gains control of the United States Senate controlling both houses of Congress.

MAY 23, 2015-The Republic of Ireland votes to legalize same- sex marriages.

NOVEMBER 5, 2016-Donald J. Trump is elected President of the United States.

APRIL 1, 2017- Bob Dylan receives the Nobel Prize for Literature at a private ceremony in Stockholm.

Looking back over the last 100 years isn't it amazing what has transpired! We have witnessed four major wars, booming economic times, depressions, harsh weather, atomic bombs, jet airplanes, landing on the moon, and computers just to name a few. I wonder what's in store for us next? Only the SHADOW knows!!

Statistically speaking only one out of every 5000 people will live to age 100. That means that we needed a sample group of 50,000 individuals for us to find 10 people who have reached the century mark.

Now, let's hear from those ten individuals who have lived and witnessed the good, the bad, and the ugly of the last one hundred years.

THESE ARE THEIR STORIES

Please Note:
Each of the stories you will read comes directly from extensive and in-depth interviews I had with each individual. In some cases, I was able to obtain additional information from family members. If any of the dates or times are not exactly accurate it could be blamed on the passage of time. One hundred years is a long time!

Arthur E. Shepard

(Born 9/21/1911)

Yes, Art Shepard was 106 years old on September 2017. He was born one year prior to the sinking of THE TITANTIC. During our conversation I asked him to what he attributed his long and healthy life. His answer was quite simple, "lead a healthy life and drink a little Jack Daniels". Art was born and grew up in Cambridge, Ohio with his mother, father and five siblings. His father, John, worked in a factory, a saloon and eventually ventured into the dry-cleaning business ultimately becoming a tailor. Art's very first memory was of a coat his father made for him when Art was in the first grade. That happened the year prior to the ending of World War I – Armistice Day – on the eleventh day of the eleventh month in 1918. Art vividly remembers the ending of the war celebrated with a parade down Wheeling Avenue in Cambridge and his father leading the band. At age 7, this was the most exciting event he had ever witnessed. It is highly

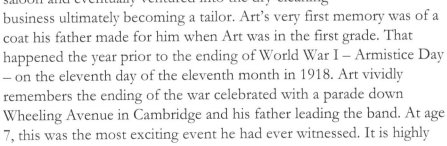

probable that Arthur Shepard is the only living person in the world today who can honestly say "I remember celebrating Armistice Day".

As a teenager during the roaring 20s, he has memories of a country gone wild with greed, prosperity and sports mania. KDKA in Pittsburgh was the first commercial radio station in the United States. In 1924, the price of a brand-new Ford automobile was $260. This was the decade of prohibition, silent movie stars, Rudolph Valentino, Lillian Gish (born in Springfield, Ohio), Al Capone, Charles Lindbergh, Joe Louis, Jack Dempsey, Babe Ruth, the New York Yankees, F. Scott Fitzgerald and Al Jolson in the first talking movie – the Jazz Singer.

All of this came to a screeching halt with the stock market crash in 1929 when Americans lost 30 billion dollars in that market. Perhaps the most dynamic decade of our countries history ended in financial disaster and economic despair. It coincided with Art's graduation from high school. Hard times to follow!!!!

Since there was no work available in Cambridge, Art decided to move to Columbus, Ohio where he lived with an aunt. His immediate concern was to get a job. Not having any contacts in town Art resorted to knocking on doors asking homeowners and businesses if they had any work for him. He simply said that he would do anything they wanted him to do and he promised to do it well. Following a lead, he eventually landed a job in January 1930 as a flunky in the advertising department of the local newspaper, The Columbus Dispatch. He worked with the Dispatch for four years until tragedy struck his family in 1934. Art's youngest brother, at age 16, died of an appendectomy in the Cambridge Hospital. His parents asked him to move back to Cambridge. He reluctantly agreed and once again needed a job. He secured a position with a company that sold gas heaters to individual

homes. He spent day after day canvassing and talking to homeowners. One of the people with whom he spoke while on his daily route was the manager of the Western and Southern Life Insurance Company. The manager asked Art if he was making any money-- the answer was a resounding "no". The manager told Arthur that with his hard work ethic if he were to enter the life insurance business he could earn an amount of money that would be commensurate with his talents.

Beginning in 1935, Art accepted a position as a debit agent with Western and Southern, not in Cambridge but in Newark, Ohio. After talking it over with his parents they agreed there was more opportunity in Newark than in Cambridge. This move was the beginning of a lifelong career as a dedicated insurance professional. Art was given a book of business of Western and Southern policyholders. His duties were to collect weekly premiums for policies in force and talk with individuals who may want to buy life insurance for burial purposes. On his very first day in the field, he sold ten life insurance policies; this was unbelievable for a novice insurance agent. In fact, his manager told Art not to tell the other agents about his success because it would be demoralizing to them. On a daily basis, Art would go about collecting ten-cents, twenty-five-cents or maybe fifty-cents to pay for a $350 death benefit policy. Please remember this was the middle of the depression. People neither had any money nor hope for the future; people struggled every day just to survive. However, with a determined attitude, Art persevered and slowly but surely, he built a successful insurance practice in Newark.

Art continued his selling activities for three years but soon tired of the weekly chore of collecting premiums. Now that he had some experience in the insurance business he opted to change companies and affiliate with a well-known insurance agency, Rankin and Rankin. It represented a reputable national company, Travelers Insurance Company. With this new relationship he could spend all his time selling larger life insurance policies, automobile insurance, homeowner's coverage, as well as property and casualty insurance. He was now in a position to talk with individuals and businesses about their total insurance needs. In order to stand out and be special Art started wearing bow ties and soon people would say, "That man with the bow tie stopped by to see you" and everybody knew it was Art- it became his "trademark". Arthur stayed with Rankin and Rankin and Travelers from 1938 to 1948. When I asked Arthur about serving in the Second World War he said that the very day he took his draft physical happened to be the day President Franklin Roosevelt died. That evening, at a poker game with his buddies at Buckeye Lake, he told his friends that because the President had passed away the armed services were not drafting any more recruits.

Art was president of the Junior Chamber of Commerce in Newark. Beginning in 1942, a group of Chamber members, to support the war effort, actually volunteered to devote four hours a day, Monday through Friday, as well as eight hours on Saturday working at Owens Corning Glass Company. They volunteered because all able-bodied 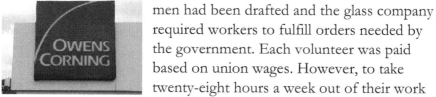 men had been drafted and the glass company required workers to fulfill orders needed by the government. Each volunteer was paid based on union wages. However, to take twenty-eight hours a week out of their work life was a tremendous sacrifice. Nevertheless, Art and his fellow colleagues felt that this was a patriotic way to serve our troops. Everyone in the country was scared and nervous about the war so this sacrifice of time away from their own livelihood seemed minor compared to the good that they were doing to save our way of life. Do you think anyone of us today would do what these men did back in 1941????

During the war years Arthur and his wife Bea had two daughters, Marcia and Lynne. This created even more financial responsibilities. Arthur was told that if he remained with Rankin and Rankin he could eventually take over the agency as one of the owners. However, the Rankins had children who were in the business and he felt that the possibility of ownership was somewhat remote. (As we all know blood is thicker than water). He knew he had to move on to greener pastures. He realized at that moment that if he wanted to own and run his own business he had to look elsewhere. Fortunately, he met Floyd Turner who made him an offer that he couldn't refuse; relocate to Columbus, Ohio and join him in an agency they would call Turner and Shepard with offices located at 22 East Gay St. Soon this Agency, affiliated with

Travelers Insurance Company, became a household name in the insurance and business community in Columbus.

In a few years they moved their agency to the Hartman Theater Building on the corner of State and Third Streets. The next move was to a building next to the Columbus Dispatch on South Third Street. Eventually in the late 60's, their final move was to the Huntington Bank Building on South High St. Their Insurance agency was thriving. By the early 70's the agency had over 60 employees. They operated in a niche market dealing almost exclusively with Professional Associations such as the Ohio Medical Association, the Ohio Dental Association and the Ohio Veterinary Association. They were also the group providers for hospitalization, life insurance and disability coverage for the Ohio Bankers Association. Their business was booming, and it was all due to the leadership provided by Floyd Turner and Art Shepard. Unfortunately, Floyd Turner did not enjoy a long life. Arthur related the story to me that on a Friday traveling by train to Ann Arbor Michigan for the annual Ohio State Michigan game they sat beside a woman who was a palm reader. She first looked at Floyd Turner's palm and said he would probably not enjoy a long life. Two years later he died of a heart attack. On the other hand, (Get it), when she studied Art's palm she saw that he had a very long life line and would enjoy a long healthy life. She was proven to be correct--Art is well over 105 years old in 2017.

Arthur, his wife and two children lived in Grandview. His daughters graduated from Grandview High School in 1956 and 1957. Unfortunately, his wife died at age 57 in the 70's. During the 50's and 60's suburbs like Grandview, Upper Arlington, Worthington, Westerville and Bexley were growing by leaps and bounds. However, downtown was still the center of commerce. Art's office was right in the middle of all the action. Banking, retailing, real estate, law firms and insurance institutions were all located within walking distance of Art's office. With his pleasing personality and knowledge of Association insurance Art was destined to become a legend!!!

A number of years after his wife Bea died, Art was playing golf at the Springfield Country Club where he was introduced to a lovely lady named Dottie Dohan. Three months later they were married, and they enjoyed many years of marital bliss. She passed away in 2013.Once again, Art was alone, but not lonely. His family and many friends keep in close touch with him. He always has much to offer and he always does it with a smile.

Arthur has devoted many hours leading charitable, business, civic and educational institutions. He is past president of First Community Church, the Ohio State University Presidents Club as well as the University Club, home of those famous sticky buns, New England clam chowder, coconut and banana cream pies. The University Club is long gone but the savory memories linger on. Art is also a member of the Scioto Country Club where everyone welcomes him as a warm and caring individual.

Art remained active in the insurance business until the early 1990s. Today, he enjoys being as he says, "just retired".

I have *personally known* Arthur Shepard for 59 years and he is one of the most remarkable persons I've ever known. From humble beginnings in Cambridge and Newark, Ohio he rose to become one of the most revered individuals in the Columbus, Ohio community. His example, gives hope to those individuals who say, "why me", "if only", "pity me". During the great depression of the 30's Art's primary concern was "SURVIVAL", but later, in a more stable economy, he set higher goals. With dogged determination and plenty of sweat and ingenuity he has made a difference in the lives of all whom he has touched. WOW! He didn't just touch people, he enveloped them.

Arthur, good job well done!!!!!!!!!!

WORDS OF WISDOM

- IF I KNEW I WAS GOING TO LIVE THIS LONG I WOULD'VE EXERCISED MORE

- I PUT FOUR KIDS THROUGH COLLEGE AND THE ONLY THING THEY DO TODAY IS SPOIL ME ROTTEN

- I CAN'T BELIEVE I'VE LIVED SO LONG – WHY ME?

- WHO COULD IMAGINE ANYONE LIVING BEYOND 100

- ONE OF THE PROBLEMS OF LIVING SO LONG IS THAT ALL OF YOUR FRIENDS ARE DEAD

Sister Edwina Devlin, OP

(Born 9/18/1914)

Edwina's family roots date back to life in Steubenville, Ohio in the 1850s. Both sets of grandparents and their children called Steubenville home. On April 30, 1902 Edwina's mother and father, Elizabeth Irwin and John Devlin were married in Steubenville. Elizabeth had four brothers and sisters and her husband John had seven siblings. Shortly after Elizabeth and John were married they took the advice of Horace Greeley who eloquently stated, "Go west, young man and grow up with the country". As a part of the Homestead Act of the late 1800s they were promised 20 acres of land in Yakima, Washington. It was an opportunity they could not resist and off they went on a five day and five-night train trip to the far west. The population of Yakima at that time was approximately 3500 people. Over the next 12 years Elizabeth and John became the parents of four children with Edwina being the youngest.

Life in Yakima, Washington

Tragically, in 1916, when Edwina was two years old, her mother passed away creating the problem of who would care for her and her siblings John, Patrick, and Anamary. Fortunately, the Catholic Schools, administered by the Jesuits, had a boarding school for boys and the Sisters of Charity, a Canadian Order, had a boarding school for girls. However, Edwina being only two years old, was too young to be admitted to the girl's boarding school. Again, fate played a hand and a friend of Edwina's mother agreed to take her in and love and care for her. From time to time her mother's friend needed to be out of town for a few days. When that occurred, she was cared for by the Sisters of Charity. Edwina roamed the halls, going from classroom to classroom, writing on all of the blackboards and becoming a total nuisance. Somehow, everyone survived.

Edwina's father, who worked for the Yakima Water Company, financially supported the children. Edwina gleefully recalls her sister dressing her in a red dress at age 2 and also people celebrating the end of World War I in 1918 when she was only four years old. What a remarkable memory going back 102 years!!

Edwina spent countless hours visiting her brothers and sisters at their respective boarding schools and because the nuns were such caring and loving individuals she decided at age 4 to become a nun. A decision she has never regretted. She remembers fondly the times that she and her siblings were able to be with their father especially on Sundays. They would take long walks through the town and the mountainsides and as a special treat they went to the local movie house for the silent movie of the week. The town of Yakima did not have a hospital or a library, but they did have a movie house. Not unusual for towns of that size.

When Edwina was six years old in 1920 her grandparents (Devlin) decided to take a trip from Steubenville to Yakima to visit their son and grandchildren. After the five-day arduous journey, they arrived in

Yakima and spent seven days visiting with the family. Unbeknownst to Edwina her father and grandparents decided that she should return to Steubenville, Ohio and live with them. On the train trip back to Steubenville her grandparents gave her a history lesson on all the members of the family as well as all of the sites as they sped by them.

Back in Steubenville Edwina was nurtured by her grandparents. seven aunts and uncles and numerous cousins. Amazingly the Devlin house had 18 rooms and to Edwina it was a mansion! She missed her brothers and sister, but again, being in a loving and caring atmosphere, life was satisfying to her. In those days there were no telephones and the only way to communicate with her family back in Yakima was by the U.S. Postal Service. Every few days she received a letter from her father and with great delight, as her grandparents read the letters to her, she loved hearing the words that her father had written. Unfortunately, her father remained in Yakima for the rest of his life.

In September 1920 Edwina attended St. Peter's Grade School in Steubenville. Incidentally, both her mother and father had attended St. Peter's. After grade school she attended Catholic Central High School where she graduated in 1932 in the depths of the depression. In September 1932 she entered the Convent – St. Mary of the Springs in Columbus, Ohio and made her first vows as a Dominican on September 18th of that year and pronounced her final vows on August 14, 1934. From 1935 to 1965, sister Edwina taught first in elementary schools and then in high schools in the Pittsburgh suburbs and in Connecticut and New York City. She taught English, Geometry, Biology and Religion. The Sisters announced in 1965 that they were going to have a mission to Peru. Sister Edwina and three other Dominicans trained for one year in Puerto Rico, then came to Peru in 1966 to begin work that continues there today. Edwina described it as a beautiful experience. She ended up teaching English to adults and teaching religion through English. She taught people like doctors, nurses and judges. They had a clinic, but the people there tended to favor those who were well – off, so she explained to them about Catholic social teaching and told you you have to help the poor- they are your brothers in Christ.

She returned to the United States in 1975 and served for the next four years as religious education coordinator at Zanesville St. Thomas Aquinas Church. She was at parishes at Marietta and Bellaire in the diocese of Steubenville from 1979 – 1988. She then worked for five years at St. Mary of the Springs to help the sisters decide what they wanted to do in retirement, also serving for part of that time as ecclesiastical notary with the Diocesan Tribunal. In 1993, sister Edwina returned to St. Thomas Aquinas in Zanesville until the year 2000.

She says "no matter where I've been, teaching has always been important to me. For 30 years, I have taught in schools along with most of the members of my congregation. As a group, we accomplished a great deal and spread interest in Catholic education".

The rest of her work involved adult education in one form or another, in Peru and then in the parishes that she served in Ohio. She found people were eager to learn more about their faith and to talk about their lives and needs and how their faith made a difference to them. She spent a lot of time listening, finding ways to help them or sending them to places that would be helpful. Sometimes, she says people just need to sit back and think "what can I do?"

Five years ago, Sister Edwina moved to the Mohun Health Care Center in Columbus, Ohio which serves retired priests and nuns, and she is its oldest resident. Her work of prayer and presence there is the latest chapter in over 80 years of service with the Dominican Sisters of St. Mary of the Springs and, since 2009, with the Dominican Sisters of Peace, a congregation formed through unifying several Dominican Communities.

Sister Edwina has simple advice for anyone who might aspire to live as long and active a life as she has: Don't worry! "I never worry," she says. "I just trust in the Lord". I believe all of us are here to do what God inspires us to do and coming to that realization brings happiness. It's been that way with me. People ask why is she so happy? She tells them, which makes them think and perhaps then they can realize how God has worked in their lives"

May Sister Edwina's life of devotion to her faith, her community, and to Catholicism be remembered as a blessing, and may she continue to serve as a model of dignity, grace and joy for us all.

Sister Edwina, may God continue to bless you and give you peace!

MORE QUOTES

- I CAN REMEMBER WHAT HAPPENED 80 YEARS AGO, BUT I CAN'T REMEMBER WHERE THE REMOTE CONTROL IS LOCATED
- OLD PEOPLE TALK ABOUT THE PAST AND YOUNG PEOPLE TALK ABOUT THE FUTURE
- OF ALL THE THINGS I'VE LOST I MISS MY MIND THE MOST
- I AM SO GLAD THAT I DON'T HAVE TO LEARN HOW TO WORK A COMPUTER
- YEARS AGO, THE MOST MEMORABLE TIME OF THE DAY WAS LISTENING TO THE SOAP OPERAS ON THE RADIO

Florence Zox

(Born 11/9/1915)

Two momentous events occurred in 1915. On May 7th, a German torpedo sank the British ocean liner Lusitania off the Irish coast, killing nearly 1200 people. On November 9th, the world welcomed its newest addition, Florence Silverman. Other than Florence there were some lesser-known people that you may remember born in the same year. Individuals like Frank Sinatra, Billie Holiday, Ingrid Bergman, David Rockefeller, Edith Piaf, Muddy Waters, Les Paul and Orson Welles. **We know their stories, now it's time to hear Florence's story.**

Florence's hometown was Chicago, Illinois for the first three months of her life. In 1915 Chicago was the second largest city in the United States with a population of approximately 250,000 people. Both her parents and grandparents were born in the United States which dates her family as citizens back to the early 1800s. However, soon after her birth the family moved to Lafayette, Indiana a small town of approximately 15,000. The move was for purely economic reasons.

Florence's grandparents owned a packaging and dry goods company and also several meat markets in and around Lafayette and they simply needed additional family members to keep the enterprise running smoothly. In February 1916, Lafayette, Indiana welcomed the Silverman family. They lived with their in-laws for three years until Florence's little sister Marjorie is born. Finally, in 1919 they moved to their own home.

World War I was over, our servicemen had returned home and now the United States was positioned to return to a robust non-war economy–**the roaring 20s have arrived.** According to Florence Lafayette, Indiana had more millionaires living in their city than any other city of its size in the United States As a youngster, Florence vividly remembers taking tennis lessons at the local country club as well as mastering the piano. She also took elocution and dancing lessons. During the summer months she attended Tripp Lake Camp for Girls located in Maine. Life was fabulous during the 1920s, especially as a teenager. The family business and the economy were thriving and then, suddenly, the world seemed to fall apart-**the stock market crash of 1929.**

The family's dry goods business and their meat markets went into a tailspin barely able to provide the family with a livable income. However, they were in the same boat with millions of other Americans who were also struggling through the great depression of the 1930s.

Florence graduated from Lafayette High School in 1933 and because her father had saved enough money for her to go to college she entered Purdue University in the fall of 1933. She chose Purdue University because her father had graduated from there and for its proximity to Lafayette. While at Purdue University Florence became engaged and was planning to be married after graduation.

However, sometimes fate enters the picture and things don't go according to plan. While attending Purdue University Florence's younger sister married and was living with her husband in Denver, Colorado. During the winter break from college in 1937 Florence traveled to visit her sister who was awaiting her first child. While in

Denver she was invited to a party and through a series of introductions she eventually met a young man, Julius Simpson Marx, known as Simpson, who was in his senior year at the Wharton School of Business at the University of Pennsylvania. Sparks started to fly. He asked her to marry him, but as we know, she was already engaged to a fellow at Purdue. Somebody had to play Solomon. Who better than Florence's father. For him the decision was easy-the boy at Purdue was not Jewish and Simpson was. He convinced Florence that having the same religious background and heritage would make the marriage more rewarding. She followed her father's advice and after graduating in June 1937 from Purdue, she and Simpson married in September of the same year at Temple Israel in Lafayette.

That is the good news of 1937. The bad news is the fact that the family business went bankrupt and her father needed employment. Fortunately, through a referral, Florence's father was able to secure a job with the Manischewitz Wine Company located in Cincinnati, Ohio. In early 1938 Florence's parents moved from Lafayette to Cincinnati Ohio. At about the same time Simpson landed a position with National Distillers located in Denver, Colorado. Simpson's territory was the western portion of the United States. Florence was ecstatic about being able to live in Denver with her husband and to be close to her sister.

As a side note, Simpson's first cousin was the famous playwright Lillian Hellman who authored The Little Foxes which debuted on Broadway in 1939 with Tallulah Bankhead starring in the original production.

Florence and Simpson's daughter Diana was born in 1939 and son Fred in 1942. During the early 1940s World War Two was in full bloom but Simpson was exempt from the service because he was married with two small children. However, Simpson felt that he needed to be a part of the war effort. In 1944 he enlisted in the Army. Sadly, while in basic training Simpson was involved in a truck accident and was killed.

Florence was a widow at age 29 with two small children. What to do? Wanting to be close to her parents she joined them in Cincinnati, Ohio. While in Cincinnati Florence became a volunteer at Jewish Hospital as a Red Cross nurse's aide which gave her a way of supporting the war effort in memory of her fallen husband. Fortunately, she was able to have people care for the children while she was doing her volunteer work. As a nurse's aide she was able to acquire many lifelong friends who remain so to this day. The war years are both a sad and rewarding time of her life.

Florence met her second husband in a very unusual way. When Florence was living in Denver (1938) she was asked to arrange a date for a young man, Morris Zox, who was visiting Denver. Florence asked her best girlfriend if she would go on a blind date with Morris. That relationship did not blossom but eight years later while living in Cincinnati she once again meets Morris, now a doctor specializing in general surgery. He lived and practiced medicine in Columbus, Ohio. The relationship clicked and in 1946 they were wed. Dr. and Mrs. Morris Zox, daughter Diana and son Fred take up permanent residence in Columbus Ohio (Bexley).

Morris was on staff at St. Anthony Hospital, Mount Caramel, White Cross and The Ohio State University Medical Center. He also was a faculty member at Ohio State. He was both an extrovert and a good storyteller – especially in Yiddish!!! If you had a story to tell Morris, he always had a better one to tell you.

On a personal note, back in January 1966 I needed an emergency appendectomy and Morris came to my rescue. That was 51 years ago, and all is well. Great surgeon.

In 1947 Florence and Morris welcomed their daughter Barbara followed by Sherry in 1949 and Laurie in 1952. The family is now complete – Florence, Morris, four daughters and a son.

Florence is a doer, not a watcher. Even while taking care of Morris and the children she knew she had to be a part of the community at large. Florence chose two organizations where she felt she could make a difference in the lives of others- HADASSAH and THE NATIONAL COUNCIL OF JEWISH WOMEN. She served as president of both the Columbus Chapter of Hadassah and the Columbus Section of The National Council of Jewish Women.

Hadassah, the Women's Zionist Organization of America. is an American Jewish volunteer women's organization. Founded in 1912 by Henrietta Szold, it is one of the largest international Jewish organizations, with 330,000 members in the United States. Hadassah raises money for community programs and health initiatives in Israel, including the Hadassah Medical Center, a leading research hospital in Israel renowned for its inclusion of and treatment for all religions and races in Jerusalem. In the US, the organization advocates on behalf of women's rights, religious autonomy and US – Israel diplomacy. In Israel, Hadassah also supports health education and research, women's initiatives, schools and programs for underprivileged youth.

The slogan for Hadassah "The Power of Women Who Do".

The National Council of Jewish Women (NCJW) is an American, volunteer – based organization that works toward social justice, improving the quality of life for families, children and women based upon principles of Judaism. At its beginning The National Council of Jewish Women focused on educating Jewish women who had lost a sense of identity with Judaism and on helping Jewish immigrants become self – sustaining in their new land. Activities include promoting education and employment for women through adult study circles, vocational training, school health programs, and free community health dispensaries. The NCJW is part of the broader effort of middle and upper-class women to assist those less fortunate. They work closely with this supplement movement epitomized by Jane Addams' Hull House in Chicago. Their work helped create the modern profession of social work. The NCJW also began a campaign for social legislation to address low – income housing, child labor, public health, food and drug regulations, and civil rights. In 1908 The National Council for Jewish Women argued for a federal anti—lynching law. They also become involved in efforts to promote world peace.

Besides her volunteering efforts and caring for the children she found time to be an avid canasta and bridge player. Years ago, she also enjoyed sewing and making clothes for her young daughters.

After the children grew up and left the household Florence and Morris moved into a high-rise condominium in the middle 1980s in Columbus, Ohio. They also wintered in Sarasota, Florida and enjoyed a great life together. Morris passed away in 2006 at age 98. Florence continues to live in their Columbus condominium. She is bright- eyed and alert and she can charm you with her winning smile. For Florence it's good to be 102 years old! For us also!

When we look at Florence's life we see a woman who loves her family, her community, her friends and anyone who needs a helping hand. Florence stays active playing bridge on a weekly basis. She has 15 grandchildren and 23 great grandchildren whom she dearly adores and who adore her. What else can a person ask for!

One final question I asked Florence "do you have any regrets?"

Her answer "no"--- life is good!

ADDITIONAL QUIPS

- IN THE SUMMER TIME, AS A CHILD, I PLAYED OUTSIDE FROM DAWN TO DUSK

- IN MY DAY, GOING TO THE MOVIES COST A DIME AND FIVE CENTS FOR A BOX OF POPCORN

- MY FAMILY LOST EVERYTHING DURING THE DEPRESSION OF THE 1930'S

- THE SECOND WORLD WAR WAS THE SCARIEST TIME OF MY LIFE

- WHEN I WAS A KID, WHITE CASTLES COST 10¢ EACH

Clara Herrman

(Born 8/28/1912)

Recently I had the opportunity to meet and have a conversation with Clara in her apartment at her assisted living residence. As I approached her she stood up so that she could give me a hug. We were perfect strangers, but I knew at that instant we were going to become great friends. What a warm and caring individual Clara Herrman is. When you have the opportunity to meet someone who is 105 years old there are two questions that come to mind. First question – "what are your earliest memories?" -- the second question –"how do you account for your longevity?" Let's take them in order.

Clara tells me that in the year 1918, at age six, she and her mother and younger brother came down with the flu which was the deadliest in modern history, infecting an estimated 500 million people worldwide, about one – third of the planet's population at that time and killing an estimated 20 to 50 million victims. **More than 25% of the U.S. population became sick, and some 675,000 Americans died**

during the pandemic. In comparison there were 623,000 deaths in the Civil War, 116,000 American deaths in World War I, 416,000 American deaths in World War II and 58,000 American deaths in the Vietnam war. In the case of the pandemic flu of 1918 / 1919 not a single bullet was fired but the devastation was unbelievable. No event in American history, which took Clara's aunt and cousin, has wiped out more people and it all happened in just one year! This Catastrophe occurred 100 years ago but Clara remembers it as if it happened just yesterday.

When it comes to our second question (longevity) Clara has a simple philosophy. "Eat lots of chocolate and stay away from doctors." She had also been doing some math homework and determined that by living 105 years her heart has beaten approximately 3.311 billion times. Clara is very proud of this fact and finds it interesting and amazing. Clara certainly is one in a billion!!!!!!

The rest of the story

Clara's grandparents were from Wales and Germany and immigrated to the Akron, Ohio area in the early 1800s. Her parents divorced when she was just a youngster and she and her little brother were raised and nurtured by her mother. During this period of her life her mother remarried, and her stepfather entered her life. He was very nice and kind and cared for her deeply. Life was good. She attended the Canton, Ohio public school system but in the second half of her junior year she decided that school was no longer important to her. She says to this day that she does not regret not graduating.

Her first job after dropping out of high school was working in a flower shop in downtown Canton, Ohio. She loved meeting the public and the few dollars that she was earning at the time. Clara also played the piano and along with a saxophone and an accordion player they formed a three-piece band that played at a local dance club on Saturday evenings. She also was a good dancer and her specialty was the Charleston. On many occasions she and her girlfriends would roll up the carpet in their living room, turn on the Victrola and dance away. This all occurred in the late 1920s – the roaring 20s.

Because of prohibition it was difficult to find alcohol for sale. Being resourceful her family decided to make their own beer. They used real glass bottles with caps and her neighbors really enjoyed consuming as many beers as possible. This enterprise was not-for-profit, it was for consumption. It seemed that everyone was making beer and thought that theirs was the best.

Finally, by 1929 the good times had come to an end. The stock market crash had plunged the economy into the Great Depression of the 1930s. Clara said that it did not affect her family because they never had any money to invest in the first place. She never felt poor because they always had everything they needed, food and a roof over their head.

LARA KEPLER HERRMAN 1912

During the depression of the 1930s the government issued coupons for items such as coffee, Crisco, flour and the other basics of life. On many occasions she would stand in line to receive a coupon which she could in turn use to acquire the necessities of life. On a few occasions they even gave out coupons for silk hosiery. To her this was a real treat.

In the early 1930s Clara met her future husband Harold and they married in 1933. Clara was almost 21 and Harold was 36. They moved to Newark, Ohio after they were married in Wheeling, West Virginia. She remembers vividly driving to and from Wheeling in her husband's Model A Ford. It was winter time and they almost froze to death but apparently their love for each other kept them warm. In 1938 they welcomed their son Philip. Clara was a stay-at-home mom and did not work outside their home until Philip started college.

Harold worked for the Ohio Power Company as well as dabbling in the jewelry business. He was transferred to Mount Vernon, Ohio but eventually moved back to Newark in 1949. Since that date Clara has been a permanent resident of Newark.

Harold served in the Army as a gun inspector before they were married. Fortunately for him his tour of duty kept him in the State of New York.

Clara Phil Harold Herrman 1946

In 1955 their son Philip graduated from Newark Catholic High School and went on to college at the University of Dayton. He wrote a book on how to become a successful investor. Unfortunately, he passed away in 2013. She has one grandson, Michael Herrman, living in Pennsylvania. He visits her each year on her birthday and he makes it a point to call her each day to wish her well. She relishes those daily calls.

Beginning in 1955 Clara worked at the downtown Newark WT Grant department store and then the John J Carroll department store. She stayed in the retail business for the next 10 years. Eventually Clara got into genealogy as a volunteer at the Newark library for almost 30 years helping people discover their ancestors. People came to the library from all over the United States wanting to find out about their families– this was a very exciting phase of Clara's life. She says it is great fun to help others discover their past.

Her beloved husband Harold passed away in 1978 and for 40 years she lived in and maintained their family home by herself. When Clara was 90 years old she was shocked when her dear friend Lori Brown asked her to accompany her on a single- engine Cessna airplane ride over Newark, Ohio. She had never been in an airplane before (and none since) and her only request was not to fly over Buckeye Lake because she was afraid of the water. This one-hour flight was both scary and exhilarating. To this day she and Lori have remained best friends. Today Clara spends her time as a resident of an assisted living facility in Granville, Ohio. She is a fellow member of the writing club as well as an expert euchre player. Clara has formed strong friendships and the residents and staff think the world of her.

Over the course of her lifetime, Clara has survived not just the 1918 flu epidemic, but also the Great Depression, countless recessions, and conflicts, including two world wars. She has seen many presidents come and go since President Wilson and she says "I am for Donald Trump. I think he'll make our best president if critics will just leave him alone". She feels that he is going to become the greatest president that ever lived.

Clara's philosophy was always to be with her husband, pay their taxes and help those who needed help the most. The world would certainly be better off if we all had the spirit, dedication and passion to make a difference in the lives of others like Clara has.

She urges that all, "pray for peace in the world, because we sure need it."

May God continue to bless you, Clara!!!

CLARA KEPLER HERRMAN 1912

Phil Herrman June 99 Newark O.

03/03/201

HUMOROUS OUTLOOK

- MY DOCTOR ASKS ME WHAT HURTS...EVERYTHING!

- IN MY NEXT LIFE I DON'T WANT ANY WRINKLES

- WHEN YOU GET TO 100, RENT A RACY MOVIE, EAT CHOCOLATES AND POPCORN AND STAY UP LATE, TIL EIGHT

- THE BEST THING ABOUT GETTING TO 100 IS THAT ALL THOSE THINGS YOU COULDN'T HAVE WHEN YOU WERE YOUNG YOU NO LONGER WANT

- AGE IS A NUMBER AND MINE IS UNLISTED

- AGE 100 – ONE MORE YEAR OF EXISTENCE DOWN THE DRAIN

Helen Bruce

(Born 10/8/1916)

Helen's mother and father were Jews living in Russia in the late 1800s. While in Russia her parents had never met but by sheer coincidence both had escaped to England in 1906. Being Jewish and living in Russia during this time period was hazardous to their very existence. It was either stay and perhaps be killed or look for a better life elsewhere. It was in London, England that Helen's mother and father met each other, fell in love and were married in 1908, the year they came to Ellis Island in New York. Between 1908 and 1922 her parents were blessed with first a son, followed by a daughter, followed by another son, followed by another daughter, followed by another son, followed by their sixth child – **Helen**. The next few years there would be another son and two daughters – a complete family, mom, dad and nine children. The family's surname was Bobrowsky. Helen changed her name to Bobrow.

When Helen's parents set foot on American soil (1908) they were greeted with some important news, significant events and key technology in their new world. For example, Henry Ford's Ford Motor Company introduced the Ford Model T costing $850. This cost was nearly 1/3 of the price of any other car on the market but still not cheap enough for the masses. Over the next few years Ford perfected assembly-line production bringing the cost down in 1916 to $368. This made it affordable to common everyday workers. It is said that "Henry Ford put the world on wheels."

1908 also witnessed the summer Olympic Games of the fourth Olympiad held in London, England and on New Year's Eve, for the first time, a ball is dropped in New York City's Times Square to signify the start of the New Year. Interesting and exciting times for a new life in America.

Immigration into the United States hit an all – time peak with 8.8 million immigrants over the decade between 1901 and 1910. The population of the United States at that time was 92,228,496 men, women and children. By 2017, the population of the United States had grown to the 323.2 million.

Welcome to the New World – The United States of America

When Helen's mother and father arrived in New York City they were able to rent a small apartment on Madison Avenue at 22nd St., not the lower East side where most immigrant families settled. With so many immigrants settling in New York, it was a challenge to make a living when her father had to clothe and feed a growing family. With little education and poor English skills Helen's father did whatever he had to do. He was able to scrape enough money together to buy a horse and wagon to peddle fruits and vegetables on the streets of Manhattan. He would go up and down the various streets and avenues and when the residences of the tenements saw him they would gather on the sidewalks and buy his produce. Eventually he had two or three permanent fruit and vegetable stands on various street corners. As small children Helen and her siblings couldn't wait for her father to come home at night so that they could count all the coins he had collected for the day. Life was difficult, but they were surviving.

Working conditions for immigrants like the Bobrowskys were deplorable. For example, on March 25, 1911 a sweat shop fire broke out at the Triangle Shirt Waist Company in Manhattan. The building was overcrowded with women and teenage girls, all immigrant workers. Safety standards were all but non – existent. The exit doors to the stairwell were locked allowing no escape from the fire on the eighth, ninth and 10th floors. The women either burned in the fire or took a chance of surviving by jumping from windows 100 feet above the street. The fire caused the death of 146 garment workers, almost all of them women. They died from the fire inside or by jumping from the windows to their death. This was life in New York City.

In 1912, with a growing family they moved to a larger apartment at 2182 Lexington Ave. Shortly after their move Helen's father created a relationship with the local A&P grocery chain in Harlem. He helped the buyers at the grocery store purchase Christmas trees during the holiday season and even picked out the best Italian wines for them to sell. As Helen told me "you did what you had to do to survive" and her father was a survivor. He told his family on numerous occasions that if you can walk from Russia (escape) to London, England you certainly can run a successful fruit and vegetable business. Helen's four brothers worked tirelessly with their father seven days a week.

When I asked Helen "what is the first thing that you remember" her reply was simple and direct "a five-cent ice cream cone". One day when she was five or six years old (1921 or 1922) her father had a nickel in his pocket and singled her out for this rare treat. That was 96 years ago, and Helen remembers it as if it were yesterday. Even today Helen says that every time she eats ice cream she thinks of her father. Such precious memories!!!!!!

Throughout the 1920s and 1930s Helen and her siblings were educated in the New York City public school system. As a teenager, Helen learned the art of ballroom dancing. She and her partner entered numerous ballroom dancing competitions in the city including the famous Commodore Ballroom built in 1917. Helen told me that if she and her partner won a particular competition they would receive a trophy and maybe five or ten dollars. She quickly added that the trophy was nice, but the money was more important. Later, the Commodore Ballroom changed its name to the now famous Empire Ballroom at the Grand Hyatt Hotel New York.

Helen graduated from high school in 1934 in the midst of the Great Depression. The 1930s saw the growth of shanty towns caused by the Great Depression, dust storms, radical politics around the world, and what many consider an upside-down world where bank robbers were seen as heroes, not villains.

After graduation from high school Helen worked for a necktie manufacturing company in Mid-Manhattan. The necktie company had recently invented a machine that would make ties that were previously made by hand. Helen was taught how to operate the machine so that she could demonstrate it to other tie manufacturers. This was the beginning of her future ventures in the clothing business.

While working at the tie manufacturing company Helen met an entertainer by the name of Lenny Kent. Lenny suggested that she should meet a singer at a local nightclub, Lee Bruce. As they say--- the rest is history. She married Lee in 1936.

In the early days of their marriage Helen felt that Lee should not pursue show business or any part of the entertainment business. Instead she urged Lee to take a job at the post office. No job could be further removed from show business.

After two years with the post office Lee needed a change of scenery. Helen and Lee had a friend who was a manufacturer's representative selling women's clothes to various department stores throughout the Mid-Atlantic states. In 1938 if you earned $25 a week you were doing well. Lee was assured that if he worked hard he could make that much or even more. Opportunity had knocked on his door. Lee represented the Princess Ann's Girls Coats Company and he traveled throughout Pennsylvania, Ohio and the State of New York. He carried his samples in the trunk of his automobile and was on the road from 4 to 6 weeks at a time. At the same time with Helen working at the necktie manufacturing company their combined incomes enabled them to be comfortable.

December 7, 1941 – the beginning of the Second World War.

Lee and Helen were attending a hockey game at Madison Square Garden on Sunday afternoon December 7, 1941 when the public-address announcer said, "will all service personnel immediately report to their stations- the Japanese have attacked Pearl Harbor". Chills ran down her spine when she saw all the service men leave Madison Square Garden. It is the worst feeling that she has ever experienced.

Helen's four brothers were drafted and served in different countries overseas during the war. By sheer coincidence, they all happened to be in London, England at the same time and were all able to meet and greet each other. When the Red Cross was informed that four brothers from the same family were reunited they set up a telephone call to the family back in New York City. The entire family was assembled to speak on the telephone to their boys. However, five minutes before the call was to be made, they were told that Winston Churchill was going to deliver a speech to the nation and that their call needed to be canceled. At least the family knew the boys were safe.

Helen and Lee's two daughters Fran and Patti were born in 1942 and 1945. Helen became a stay at home mother for her two daughters because in those days women who had small children did not work outside the home.

In 1954 Helen and Lee moved from New York City to University Heights in Cleveland, Ohio. Now that the children were a little bit older Helen joined her husband selling girls outerwear on the road. Helen's mother would travel from New York to Cleveland to care for her daughters while they were both away. Helen told me that her mother once said to her "when your husband wants or needs you there, you should go". Helen loved traveling with Lee to the many trade shows to see what was new in the clothing business. With a twinkle in her eye she told me "I loved people, I loved selling and I was really good at it".

Eventually they retired and relocated to Hallandale, Florida in 1977. Helen and Lee celebrated their 50th wedding anniversary in March 1986 but one month later Lee passed away. Helen lived in Florida for 32 years. At age 89 her daughter suggested she move to Columbus, Ohio so that she could see her great – grandchildren growing up.

Helen has four grand – children and nine great- grandchildren. She has one great grandchild who is age 20 and she says it "frightens me". She said she can't believe she has lived so long. Helen also laments that she is the last surviving sibling in her family.

Helen's parents fled from Russia just as other families fled from Germany, Italy, Ireland and the Baltic states to seek a better life in the United States. The prejudice and racism that was rampant in those countries during the turn of the 20th century left little or no options – stay and be killed or flee with a chance to survive and be free.

Lucky for us, Helen, that you are a survivor!

In memoriam

Sadly, Helen passed away on January 29, 2018. She lived a long and meaningful life and the good deeds she accomplished along the way will be remembered by all who knew her. May she rest in peace.

PRECIOUS MEMORIES

- WHATEVER HAPPENED TO THOSE RED SOLED BLACK AND WHITE SADDLE SHOES?
- YOUTH IS WASTED ON THE YOUNG
- I WISH I COULD REMEMBER THE NAMES OF ALL OF MY GRAND AND GREAT GRANDCHILDREN
- FRANKLIN ROOSEVELT WAS THE LAST GREAT PRESIDENT OF THE UNITED STATES
- I HAVE NO FIVE-YEAR PLAN

Robert Main

(Born 3/21/1917)

At the very first conversation I had with Bob I inquired "what are your earliest memories as a child?" His response was immediate -the love of my parents, especially my mother. He shared with me a paper that he had written some years ago entitled **"Why My Mom Was the Greatest."**

"In 1916, Curtis Main, a young farmer, got tired of driving his horse and buggy five miles on cold nights to court a lovely farm girl, Catherine Vergon. So, they got married. In 1917, son Bob arrived at the Jane M. Case Hospital in Delaware, Ohio.

This story still disturbs me: I still wonder how dad could haul his pregnant wife in a jostling buggy on a rough, frozen unpaved country road six miles long in March 1917! For your friends who have questioned my mental capacity now you have a clue. And, perhaps dad's buggy ride was the greatest, too!

Note of explanation: the Main farm was located on the Marion Road, now US Route 23. However, in 1917, the road was gravel and dirt. Cars were being introduced in about 1913. Finally, the old road became Ohio's second highway in 1924.

In my mind, mother exemplified the attributes of loving and sharing. She cared for everything that lived and was responsible for her possessions. She helped us to plan, manage, work, and sacrifice on the farm. Also, she accepted opportunities to reach out and help the less fortunate whenever she was able.

She raised chickens and turkeys; gathered fresh eggs to exchange for groceries. She was dad's shopper and delivery woman for special farmer needs, such as hardware items, implement repair parts, medication for livestock. She ran errands for her mother and her mother's sister on the next farm. She was my nurse and coach: also delivered lemonade and sugar bread to dad and me while we cultivated and harvested on the sweltering summer days. She guided me through school — — — what a task!

Since my family members had not attended college, I was reluctant to enroll knowing that my dad needed my help on the farm. The great depression had left him with a heavy mortgage. Mother advised, "College is becoming more important. Such training is a good thing. So, follow your heart." And God made it so!

While performing the above tasks, mom served dad, and the seasonal handyman, in our home without the following conveniences: electricity, refrigeration, indoor plumbing, self – fueled cook stove, automatic heating/cooling, and no home help. In addition, she kept an orderly home and cooked on a wood stove.

On Monday, the weekly wash day, water was pumped from the underground cistern, and heated in a boiler on the stove, then carried to the washing machine on the back porch. The operating power was a small portable gasoline engine pulled from the pump at the barn. The cistern received rainwater from the roof. It also received soot in cold weather from coal heating.

Finally, in 1933, electricity reached our farm. This was a great improvement if one had the funds to wire the house and buy electric appliances.

This dear mom, who had given me her best of everything, left this note in her Bible, "Robert, the happiest two days of my life were when you were born and when you married Phyllis. She is tops!"

Mother was committed to loving God and demonstrated it by loving her neighbor as she did her husband and son. Indeed, she was humble and great!"

Don't we now have a better understanding of what rural and farm life was like in Ohio, especially during the 1920s and the depression years of the 1930s! I know I do.

Let us chronicle the life of a truly honorable man –BOB MAIN!!!

As a youngster Bob attended a one – room schoolhouse, Schaaf, for the first three grades. There were seven students, five from one family. It was located 1.2 miles from Bob's home; was heated by a coal stove. Water came from a hand –pump; outhouses, of course, were the outside toilets. During his middle school years his school merged with another Township school and the enrollment rose to twelve. Eight of the grades were taught by one teacher. Needless to say, he either walked to school, rode his bicycle or on special occasions, with weather permitting, he rode his pony which delighted all the other children. During that time weather was not an excuse for missing school – no snow days! In 1930 – the end of his seven years in country schools, he enrolled in the college preparatory curriculum at the new Frank B. Willis High School in Delaware, Ohio.

Every day, before going to school, Bob had farm chores to complete. Life on the farm when he was young, was without mechanical equipment, especially a tractor. All land was tillable by hand – pure drudgery. In 1927 when Bob was ten years old his father was able to buy a Ford tractor, a life saver from back breaking labor. When Bob was twelve or thirteen years old, as a small boy, he had to manhandle the tractor since it had no hydraulics. This was a Herculean effort, but he finally mastered it through sheer determination. This is a trait he has relied upon for his entire lifetime.

In1929, when Bob was 12 years old, the world came to a screeching halt with the historic stock market crash followed by the Great Depression of the 1930s. Bob tells me "the depression was hell". The entire family was under constant worry and pressure to keep from losing their farm to foreclosure. To keep their farm intact his father borrowed $1000 from a local bank which was a monumental amount of money in those days. Bob says that some way or somehow his dad was able to pay off that loan. Many farmers were unable to pay their debts and lost everything. A sad and desperate time for Americans in the 1930s.

In 1934 Bob became a graduate of the Frank B. Willis High School in Delaware, Ohio. After graduating high school, he felt an obligation and love of his family to work side-by-side with his father. However, his mother insisted that he pursue a college education. In the fall of 1934 he enrolled as a freshman at Ohio Wesleyan University in Delaware, Ohio which was the training ground for Methodist ministers and teachers. Knowing that he did not want to be a teacher or a minister, in the fall of 1935 he transferred to The Ohio State University in the School of Agricultural Engineering. He had determined that agriculture and mechanical engineering were two subjects about which he was passionate.

At that time, he had very little cash, but two generous professors employed him as a draftsman for thirty-five cents per hour. Bob also realized that for him to become successful in later life he would need to learn communication skills. To that end he sold personal – fit ladies' Real Silk Hosiery and men's socks door – to – door. The Real Silk Hosiery Mills in Indianapolis was a quality company which taught an honorable selling method. The money earned made the difference between him staying in college or dropping out and going back to the farm.

In his junior year at Ohio State he met and fell in love with a co-ed, Phyllis Tinling. She also was in the College of Agriculture at Ohio State. As a senior Phyllis was nominated for senior class president – the first woman to be nominated for the top campus office.

In the spring of 1939 Bob and Phyllis graduated from OSU. Bob told me "the Lord provided both of them with jobs for college and marriage in 1941, post – depression years."

From 1939 –1942 Bob was the farm market analyst for the Armco Steel Corporation. He had been recommended by his OSU professors. His starting salary was $140 per month. In 1941, the attack on Pearl Harbor changed their lives. The National Service draft followed.

Bob strongly believed that the war would be shortened if servicemen would be assigned to billets to which they were best qualified. He decided he needed to be a commissioned officer! So, he prepared a personal resume of his education and work experience since age twelve. Without assistance or direction, Bob rode the train to D.C. and a taxi to the Naval Department. He canvassed each bureau; indeed, every officer listened intently and questioned his purpose. The last one asked him to repeat his story. Then he replied, "Main, I believe you really are sincere! You'll hear from me." Soon Bob received a letter from the Navy with his appointment as an Ensign. Next, Bob's orders arrived directing him to the Navy training school at Princeton University. Three weeks later, the Navy announced that the new amphibious force was under construction, and, 90% of his class would be assigned to it. Further, they should consider themselves expendable.

After leaving Princeton University Bob became an engineering officer of an LCI, known as a landing craft infantry in the Pacific. The landing craft infantry were several classes of seagoing amphibious assault ships of the Second World War used to land large numbers of infantry directly onto beaches. They were developed in response to a British request for a vessel capable of carrying and landing substantially more troops than their smaller landing craft assault vehicles could handle. The result was a small steel ship that could land 200 troops traveling from rear bases on its own bottom at a speed of up to 15 knots. He participated in the amphibious landings on the Marshall and Marianas Islands. He was discharged in November 1945 with two stripes. Job well done!!

From 1939 to 1987, Bob was employed by various companies in sales and marketing management positions. Working at NIBCO in Elkhart, Indiana, Bob was appointed director of long-range corporate planning.

Back tracking a little, after 29 happy years together, and with two children entering college, life turned to a serious track as

Phyllis began her 17-year struggle with Alzheimer's disease and cancer. Bob and Phyllis weathered those last years together until her death in 1987. Good would come even in death, though, as doctors studied Phyllis's brain to gain insights into the disease which claimed her life. Her eyes have been used to restore sight through the Lion's Eye Bank Service.

In 1987 Bob retired. God would soon ease Bob's loss with a new companion, Jean Gilmore who had gone through the same tests of faith with her husband Bill, who died after an eight-year struggle with heart problems. Unfortunately, Jean passed away in 2008. The combined families together have six children, plus four spouses – two children and 10 grandchildren spread over five states.

Bob Main has devoted his life to serving others

In a congressional resolution in honor of Bob on the occasion of his induction into the Central Ohio Senior Citizens Hall of Fame, Deborah Price, a member of Congress states that Bob continues to undertake the noble effort of participating in the numerous philanthropic organizations dealing with Alzheimer's disease, acting as a co – leader of a husband's support group. Committed to the spiritual ministry of the international Gideons, Bob also volunteered in the prison ministry at the Ohio Correction Reception Center in Orient, Ohio.

John Glenn, United States Senator, also congratulated Bob as the newest member of the Central Ohio Senior Citizens Hall of Fame in 1995.

Today Bob is at peace with the world. Despite the personal hurts from his father's drinking, parents' scuffling, farm indebtedness, great depression, parents' divorce, struggle for college funds, post – graduation debt, etc. the Lord has led him to a happy life. He defended our country against the Japanese in World War II, was a devoted husband and has set high standards of conduct for his children and grandchildren. He is a person we should all try to emulate.

Bob, may God continue to bless you.

THE MAIN FAMILY
Front row: Ken Reim, Jean Main, Bruce Main.
Second row: Kathy Reim, Karya Reim, Kevin Reim, Cari Main, Bob Main, Jeff Main, and Cathy Main.

Bob at the left and his cousin, John Howard Law. John was Bob's only close-by playmate.

Bob and Phyllis - one of
their last pictures together.

Bob Kevin, Next Bob,
Kathy Reim's husband and
Karyn,

MORE THOUGHTS

- BOY, COULD FRED ASTAIRE AND GINGER ROGERS DANCE

- LIFE IS SIMPLE, IT'S JUST NOT EASY

- WHY DOES EVERYONE NEED TO CARRY AROUND A CELL
  PHONE?

- TODAY'S CARS HAVE TOO MANY BUTTONS

- PEOPLE NEED TO TALK MORE AND TEXT LESS

Virginia Ann Fulcomer

(Born 10/11/1916)

It was a bright, crisp, sunny fall day Wednesday, October 11, 1916 when the world, with a full moon as a beacon, welcomed its newest addition – Virginia Rohlf.

THIS IS HER STORY

Virginia's father's parents were from Germany, moved to Chicago, then to Minnesota where her great grandfather's three sons each were granted homesteads under the Homestead Act of 1862. Homesteads had poor roads – and the people had a hard time getting around – before cars. The farm needed to be self-sufficient, so they had their own smokehouse, water supply, machine shed, barn, and ice houses filled with frozen blocks cut from nearby Rush Lake. The farm had a huge garden and fruit trees. Food was preserved. Everyone contributed work.

Her mother's parents could be called "Yankees" – her ancestors on her mother's side go back to the Mayflower. Two notable ancestors are John Brown, the abolitionist and William Denison, who in 1853, pledged $10,000 to the Granville, Ohio Literary and Theological Institution. In recognition of that $10,000 gift the trustees changed the name of the institution to Denison University. Virginia's mother was a schoolteacher and boarded at her father's parent's home. Her mother went directly from grade school to the University of Minnesota as was possible in those days. She graduated as a teacher and taught for 10 years before marrying.

Her father attended the St. Paul Business School while also learning the plaster and cement business in St. Paul. Her parents were married in 1913 and Virginia's brother, Harley, was born a year later. For the first few years they lived on a farm where her father built up his cement work business and a hired man did the farm work. In a few years they moved to the nearby town of Rush City, a town of 1100 inhabitants, about sixty miles north of St. Paul and a mere four miles from Wisconsin.

When Virginia was not quite five years old, one of the school teachers became ill and couldn't fulfill her contract. Virginia's mother was asked to teach that year (married women were not usually allowed to teach.) Her mother said she would teach if Virginia could enter school a year early. When Virginia was in the third grade the third and fourth grade students were in the same room. The teacher noticed that she was doing the fourth-grade work, so she was moved to the higher grade. To this day she is the youngest person (age 15) to graduate from Rush City High School.

I asked Virginia "what is one of the first things that you remember?" She related that on September 14, 1923 her father bought a crystal set radio so that he could listen to the heavyweight prizefight featuring Luis Firpo of Argentina versus Jack Dempsey. Firpo knocked Dempsey out of the ring in round two but Dempsey was able to climb back in before the 10-count rule would have awarded the heavyweight championship to Firpo. Infuriated, Dempsey knocked out Firpo at the end of that second round to retain the world's heavyweight championship. Virginia said her father was extremely pleased and excited with the outcome. What memories.

For transportation in those days, her father had a Ford Model T truck that he used in the cement business and a Ford Model T car for the family. In 1929, he bought a Model A Ford and Virginia, at age 13, drove it often. In those days it wasn't necessary to take a driver's education course or even have a driver's license. As you might suspect there were also no seat belt laws.

After graduating from high school there was no money for college, so she helped care for her mother who would become an invalid. She continued to study piano (which was paid for in cement services), took classes in typing and shorthand, worked part time at local businesses and was very active in church activities. The year was 1932 and here comes bad economic times.

The depression (1929-1941) originated in the United States after a major fall in stock prices with the news of the stock market crash of October 29, 1929. Between 1929 and 1932 worldwide gross domestic product (GDP) fell by an estimated 15%. For example, the Ford automobile company's auto sales declined by fifty percent in 1932. By comparison, worldwide GDP fell by less than 1% during the recession of 2008 and 2009. The great depression had devastating effects in countries both rich and poor. Personal income, tax revenue, profits and prices dropped, while international trade plunged by more than 50%.

Unemployment in the United States rose to 25% and in some countries rose as high as 33%. Farming communities and rural areas where Virginia and her family lived suffered as crop prices fell by about 60%. Facing plummeting demand with few alternative sources of jobs, areas dependent on primary sector industries such as mining and logging suffered the most. By mid – 1930, interest rates had dropped to low levels, but expected deflation and the continuing reluctance of people to borrow meant that consumer spending and investments were depressed. This downward spiral of the economy lasted until the United States declared war on Japan in 1941.

During the depression Virginia's family never complained about the lack of money. Everyone was poor – but busy and doing the best they could. Much of the payment for work her father did was in usable goods or bartered services. The bleak times where accented by terrible dust storms that devastated the land, mainly in the mid and southwestern states. Individuals who lived during this period as teenagers or young adults can testify to the total despair created by the depression. The mood of the country was just plain somber. There seemed to be no hope for the future.

The country needed somebody or something to help change the human soul, mind and spirit in those dire times. They simply needed an escape from reality. Fortunately, beginning in 1933 those fabulous "Hollywood musicals" came to our rescue. For an admission fee of fifteen cents, plus a nickel for a box of popcorn you could transport yourself away from the cares of the day and live in a fantasy world of the glamorous rich and famous. A couple of hours in a movie house in those days was time well spent to lift one's spirits. Virginia and her friends loved going to the movie house as an escape from reality. Experiencing the movies was like having a bowl of chicken soup to cure your cold. The soup probably didn't cure your cold, but it sure did taste good.

Let's take a look at the
GOLDEN AGE OF HOLLYWOOD MUSICALS
of the 1930s and those stars who lit up the screen.

"Gold Diggers of 1933"	1933
"42nd St."	1933
"The Gay Divorcee"	1934
"Top Hat"	1935
"Swing Time"	1936
"The Great Ziegfeld"	1936
"The Wizard of Oz"	1939

The movie stars who brought these musicals to life reads like a Who's Who in Hollywood history – – –

Judy Garland, Ray Bolger, Ginger Rogers, Billy Gilbert, Joan Blondell, Edward Everett Horton, James Cagney, Jeanette MacDonald, Myrna Loy, Fred Astaire, Oliver Hardy, Stan Laurel and never to be forgotten the Marx Brothers and the Three Stooges .

Each person that I have spoken with seemed to echo the same thoughts when they look back to the late 1920s and all of the 1930s- "We lived through it and we are still here".

During the mid-1930s Virginia met her future husband Charles, a student pastor from Macalester College in St. Paul. They were married in 1938. They founded a loving partnership which lasted into its 65th year. Their three children, Judith, Cheryl and Mark, in turn, gave them five grandchildren who now are parents of nine great grandchildren. (25 children, grandchildren, great grandchildren and in-laws get together at Fountain Point in Michigan each summer for a most enjoyable time).

While Charles studied at McCormick Seminary in Chicago, Virginia worked at the large Montgomery Ward mail order establishment on the Chicago River which employed around fifteen hundred people. She started in the lowly position of order clerk but soon became the department file clerk, then payroll supervisor, and soon she was promoted to the personnel department as the personal auditor responsible for certifying that all employees had the proper classification, training, and salary so that the company would not be in trouble with the rising labor unions.

In the years that followed, Virginia and Charles raised their three children and worked together in ministry in Indiana, Wisconsin, Portland, Oregon, Los Angeles and Ohio. Virginia enrolled part time in college classes along the way until the children were in school and at that time she and Charles decided she should attend UCLA and finish her degree.

Virginia received her bachelor's degree in psychology from UCLA and her master's degree in psychology from Westminster College in Pennsylvania. At that time the college needed someone to teach psychology and they chose her. During her first year as a teacher, the owner of S.S. Kresge discount stores provided a grant for 10 people to start a Ph.D. program. Through a testing process Virginia was one of the candidates chosen. She received her Ph.D. degree in psychology from Western Reserve (Case Western Reserve today). Her research and dissertation for her doctorate degree was on the subject "Children's school behavior and their perceptions of home experiences". It examined the relationship between over and under achievement and/or shy – withdrawn or aggressive problematic behavior and a child's perceived relationship with her/his parents.

One of the areas that she was most interested in was the Rorschach test (inkblots) and apperception testing. In 1962 she met Dr. Zucker who was running the Youngstown Child Guidance Center. Virginia joined forces with Dr. Zucker and soon became the head psychologist and director of the psychological services for the agency. She also had a private practice at the same time. She was both busy and involved.

During this period, she was one of two psychologists to take part in a Youngstown school research project titled, MOTIVEMENT CENTERS, designed to determine if being provided an abundance of especially interesting study materials and needed psychological services would turn underachievers into achievers. The project was very successful and enabled her to be credentialed as a school psychologist in addition to being licensed as a clinical psychologist. This work meant that she could have a mini – clinic in each school to which she was assigned and could work with parents and teachers as well as the children to whatever extent was needed. This truly was for what she was suited, and she finished her career in private practice in the most enjoyable fashion.

As Virginia's husband got transferred around the country she was always there to support him. She had no personal plans, never applied for a job, but opportunities always presented themselves to her. As she told me "he went, I followed, things happened".

Throughout the 1970s, 80s and 90s Virginia and Charles traveled extensively. They visited fifty-two countries and twenty-one islands. They have been to Northern Ireland six times, England ten times, France four times, Switzerland twice, Greece three times, New Zealand twice, Spain two times as well as Fiji, Puerto Rico, Cyprus, Jamaica and Granada. The majority of these trips were for either psychological or religious conferences.

Unfortunately, Charles entered a nursing home in 2000 and passed away in 2003. Virginia continues a healthy and productive life. Back in the year 2000 she wrote a 100-page e-book titled THE BOLD FAITH IN THE NEW CENTURY. It was meant to convey her religious beliefs to her family and friends. Recently she has written a short e-book which proposes changes in Christianity. It is entitled BACK TO THE WORD: A NEW REFORMATION and is accessible on the web: www.backtothelivingword.com

Once again, I have had the privilege to meet a truly remarkable individual. She is a phenomenally brilliant and caring person whose life had brought meaning to those she has touched. Her work has helped literally thousands of individuals both young and old to be able to live up to their God-given potentials.

Virginia, a life well lived---May you enjoy many additional years helping others!!!

SAYINGS

- I WISH MY GRANDCHILDREN WOULD CALL ME MORE OFTEN

- I REMEMBER WHEN A NICKEL BOUGHT A NICKEL'S WORTH

- I WISH I COULD ONLY REMEMBER THE GOOD TIMES

- I AM FINALLY GETTING USED TO THE FACT THAT I AM GETTING OLD

- MY DOCTOR TELLS ME I WILL LIVE FOREVER – I'M NOW LOOKING FOR A NEW DOCTOR

Charlotte Gallant

(Born 7/27/1917)

Two memorable events occurred in 1917. On April 2, President Woodrow Wilson asked the U.S. Congress for a declaration of war on Germany and on July 27th Blanche and Ellis Gallant welcomed Charlotte as the newest addition to their family. Their home was located at 236 N. Washington St. in Delaware, Ohio. The house dates back to the early 1900s and still stands today. Joining the family were two brothers Ellis and Tom. The family has deep roots in Ohio. Charlotte's grandparents on both her mother's and father's side were Ohioans. Her mother's family lived in Plain City and her father's parents are from Alexandria.

Growing up in Delaware, Ohio

As a child, living in a small town like Delaware had some tremendous advantages. Charlotte could roam around town without her parents worrying about her safety. Everyone seemed to know everybody else's names as well as where they worked, where they lived and where they attended church. You just can't keep many secrets living in a small town like Delaware, Ohio. Even as a youngster Charlotte felt a sense of community which she has embraced for her entire lifetime. Having a loving family and community has given her the strength to achieve her lifetime goals.

Charlotte's father was an integral part of the community. First, serving as a salesman, he provided stationary supplies to various small businesses in Delaware County followed by working in the Delaware US Postal Service. If you worked at the post office you automatically knew everybody's name in town and they knew yours. He also was a partner in the Hardin and Gallant bookstore in downtown Delaware.

I asked Charlotte for any early remembrances. She had two… When she was four years old in 1921 she was visiting her grandmother and apparently she was making a great deal of noise and her grandmother used a switch on the back of her legs. Charlotte was shocked. She had been disciplined from time to time but never spanked and having her grandmother strike her was upsetting. That episode happened 97 years ago but she has never forgotten. Wow!!!!

She also remembers, at about the same age, she caught her finger in their back-porch screen door and started screaming. Charlotte's mother thought that she was squealing because she was mad, not injured. Her mother quickly realized that she had cut her finger and bandaged it. Her mother apologized for yelling at her and all was forgiven. Again, a traumatic event long remembered.

Charlotte attended grade school (North School) in 1923 which conveniently was located a few doors away from their home on N. Washington St. Her high school years were spent at Delaware Willis High School graduating in 1935 in the middle of the depression. Times were bleak during the depression years, but the family had a steady source of income as a result of her father having a civil service position with the US Postal Service and with her grandparents owning farms they had a steady supply of fruits, vegetables, dairy products and meats.

After completing high school Charlotte enrolled at Ohio Wesleyan College graduating in 1939 with a degree in history. Unfortunately, she was unable to find employment and  as a result she enrolled at The Ohio State University and received a degree in German. Subsequently she received a bachelor's degree in Library Science from Case Western Reserve and Library Science has been her life's work since the 1940s.

During World War II Charlotte became the librarian at Delaware Willis High School before moving, in 1946, to Cleveland, Ohio where she worked at the Cuyahoga County Public Libraries. A part of her duties was to travel to various schools within Cuyahoga County as a librarian. However, as the years passed, eventually each school had their own library and as a result Charlotte's only traveling was to the various branches for the rest of her library career in Cleveland. She officially retired in 1980 and moved back to Delaware, Ohio.

Retirement years-Volunteering and Traveling

Volunteering: Once Charlotte retired she spent her entire life and devotion to volunteering in the Delaware community. In 1995 she decided that after 15 years of volunteering it was time to move on and let others serve the community. That year she received the Volunteer of the Year award from the Chamber of Commerce of Delaware, Ohio. A befitting tribute to a person who really cares!

Traveling: During Charlotte's working years she attended many library science conventions throughout the country which she thoroughly enjoyed. She loved meeting other librarians from all parts of the United States. Once retired she took a train trip traveling throughout the United States but, her most memorable trips were to China, Japan, Egypt, Morocco and Marrakesh with her niece Kathy Nutt. What memories.

When her father passed away in 1971 she inherited 83 acres of farmland which she donated to the Preservation Parks of Delaware County-Gallant Farm. The Preservation Parks protects what

matters--natural and historic features of Delaware County. The park district is committed to preserving their natural areas: places where wildlife can find what they need to live, and places where people can find an oasis of quiet in the midst of a busy life. In a recent program held at Gallant Farm families were able to tour the farmhouse, help make cider, meet the animals and enjoy traditional games. It was suggested that ladies wear their best "going – to – town" hat and if they did they may win a prize. They also suggested that you bring an item that you would like to include in a time capsule which would be opened in 25 years.

Charlotte emphasized that when she graduated from college her limited options were to become either a teacher or a nurse. She feels that women were more discriminated against in her day than today. Today she sees the opportunities are limitless of what a young woman coming out of school can pursue. Her advice is that the younger generation should take advantage of all opportunities.

I asked her if she had a goal to become 100 and she says it never was an issue. However, she added that once she got into her late 90s she changed her mind. She thought it might be great to reach 100. However, today she admits that being 100 is really no fun. She states that old age comes with the territory. She laments the fact of her failing eyesight and having to rely on others to help her from time to time. She never wants to be a hindrance to others. I'm sure she isn't.

Finally, I asked Charlotte what she feels is the secret to her long life. Without hesitation she said, "I was born thin" and I continued to be thin for my entire 100 years. If that is the secret, I am going on a diet.

Charlotte Gallant, who never married, is one of the most personable and intelligent individuals that I have ever met. She has devoted her entire lifetime to education and volunteerism. She is a model citizen – a person we should emulate.

Charlotte, may your legacy of giving and sharing live on forever!

FERTILE MINDS

- TODAY, EVEN MY KIDS ARE OLD

- I WISH SOMEONE COULD EXPLAIN WHAT WI-FI IS ALL ABOUT

- LIFE IS LIKE A ROLL OF TOILET PAPER, AS YOU GET TO THE END IT GOES FASTER

- LIFE GOES SO FAST – IT IS AS IF I AM HAVING BREAKFAST EVERY 20 MINUTES

- I LOVE SPEAKING WITH YOUNG PEOPLE – THEY HAVE SHORTER STORIES

George (Bud) Patch

(Born 8/30 /1917)

Bud Patch was born on the family farm in Plain City, Ohio the same year the United States entered World War I. His immediate family included his mother Ruth, father Jay and three siblings Alice, Earl and Betty. They worked hard each and every day from dawn to dusk to eke out a living as farmers. Times were especially bleak during the depression years of the 1930s. When Bud was a freshman in high school he was urged by his father to drop out of school and work full-time on the farm. It was a fact that unless he could spend full time with his father working the crops and livestock, the farm would be lost, and they would have no other source of income. His father did not own the farm, he was a sharecropper. As we know in those days there were no government assistance programs, no entitlements. It was the survival of the fittest and Bud and his family faced the situation head-on. Bud worked with his father from 1932 to 1952. They had survived both the depression and the rationing that went along with the shortages in World War II. In 1942, Bud had passed his physical to enter the armed services but was classified as 4F. His draft board decided that the country needed farmers as well as fighters, so he remained a farmer and has done so for his entire lifetime.

One of the first questions that I asked Bud "what is the first thing that you remember?" He immediately responded that in 1920 when he was age three he fondly remembers his little sister being born. He said his whole family was so excited. All he knew was that now he had a little sister to play with.

From the day he could do chores on the farm as a youngster, his life has been connected in one way or another with farming and animals. In those early days

plowing and field work was done by hand. He and his father farmed 235 acres which was back breaking work. In order to keep various items cool he remembers their ice house where they stored ice cut from the Scioto River. There were no refrigerators or electricity on the farm. Life was bleak but they all survived.

A self-made man

Bud & Helen Patch

Bud and his wife Helen eloped to Kentucky and were married on May 22, 1940. They didn't inform Helen's parents for fear that they would not approve of the marriage. It took them a year to work up the courage to tell her parents they were married. Their fears were unfounded – as they were congratulated and welcomed to the family. That hurdle had been crossed. Over the next few years Bud and Helen welcomed four children of whom Terry and Buddy survive today. Their daughters have passed away; Linda died of a brain tumor and Virginia succumbed to cancer.

Throughout their first 14 years of marriage Bud and Helen lived in a number of houses. However, in 1954, Bud purchased 50 acres of land on Home Road with a mailing address of Delaware, Ohio. He was now ready, willing and able, to build his dream farm house. Without a set of blueprints or architectural drawings he built the entire home himself doing all of the plumbing and electrical work. He must have done a fabulous job of construction because the family home still looks beautiful some 64 years later.

On their farm, aside from growing many different crops and large gardens of vegetables, flowers and many kinds of trees, they raised exotic animals such as buffalo, beefalo, ostrich, emu, rhea, llama, alpaca, Persian pigs, and chesants (a cross between a chicken and a pheasant). Bud also had every kind of domestic animal. He even had porcupines at one time and of course he built four ponds with many varieties of fish. He still has rabbits, swans, geese, peacocks, chickens,

goats and deer on the farm today. We couldn't go on without mentioning that he had many hunting dogs over his lifespan. For fun, Bud did his share of hunting and fishing. Groups of his friends would journey up to Lake Erie, Indian Lake, Florida, out west, and other such places to enjoy their sport. As a taxidermist a number of fish adorn his home. Although he went deer, bear and elk hunting, his main love was fishing. He and his friends went to Canada and portaged to the remote fishing lakes. They hand carried their boat to these lakes. Bud was well known in the neighborhood for his fishing parties where they would cook the fish they caught, and the neighbors would bring some food which turned into a great potluck meal. You might have even found a few people playing their favorite card game, euchre. Bud also ran a maple sugar camp every year. All of the family, neighbors and friends would volunteer to help gather and boil down the syrup. This wasn't so much a moneymaker as it was a winter get-together. There was always great food and fellowship connected with the Patch family.

Bud has always been a restless man looking for new challenges. Besides his farm duties his entrepreneurial talents created great opportunities for him and the people he served. Let me give you some examples:

He was a firefighter for the Delaware Concord Township. On two occasions he administered CPR and saved both lives. He also ran the snow trucks during the winters.

He worked as a subcontractor working on construction and welding projects that took him all over the United States and in many different types of manufacturing companies. He had the mind of a mechanical engineer. He could fix anything from a tractor to an airplane engine.

He had his own trucking company. His slogan was "have truck will travel" meaning that with his truck he would get the load to its destination on time. He did work for a moving company, American Van Lines but he didn't own it.

He is a government certified dynamite expert. On many occasions farmers contracted with him to dynamite tree stumps in their farm fields. He not only dynamited them but also hauled away the debris.

He was a welder, operated heavy equipment, did landscaping and was a metal fabricator.

He contracted with a Quarry to cut and deliver flag stone and huge rocks and boulders to various projects like golf courses and commercial buildings. In many cases he designed and built flagstone patios and walls for the finest homes and businesses in Central Ohio.

The social aspect of Bud consisted of him becoming a 32nd degree Mason. As a 50-year member he served in several offices and as Worshipful Master. Being the good Mason, Bud also was a member of Eastern Star along with his wife Helen. What a great partnership in service to others.

In the early 1970s he sold some acreage he owned in the Dublin, Ohio area on Concord Rd near Muirfield Village Golf Course. This was one financial deal that really worked out well for him.

In the middle 1980s he purchased a home in central Florida so that he and his wife could enjoy their retirement years. However, Bud became very restless and decided that he was not ready to retire and just vegetate. They returned to their farm in Delaware and back to work he went. He started getting serious about his metal art in his 80s starting out with small figures/plaques to put inside of the house, like swans or doves. He progressed and started making imaginary birds out of old machinery parts, shovels, rakes and old bicycles. He made sculptures from old metal wagon wheels and bicycles. He also started making animal sculptures – giraffes, squirrels, owls and pigs. Eventually he made Halloween items like cats with their hair raised on their backs and carved pumpkins. Finally, he made life-size people images including his version of a selfie that greets guests as they drive down his driveway before meeting the large and menacing looking dinosaurs that appear ready to jump out at you.

Bud & Helen 50th Wedding Anniversary

In May 1990 Bud and Helen celebrated their 50th wedding anniversary with their family (a total of seventeen children, grandchildren and great-grandchildren). In 2003, after 63 years of marital bliss, Helen passed away. A sad time for the entire family and extended community. At age 99 Bud finally did retire. Today he enjoys his family and new friends he has met at the assisted living facility where he resides.

Truly Bud Patch is a man for all seasons. Without a formal education he has attained tremendous success in his life's work as a farmer, sculptor, mechanical genius, animal lover, mentor and a service provider to others. His "get it done" attitude is an inspiration to all of us!

Bud, you certainly have made a difference in the lives of those people you have touched. You are a treasure to behold!

Bud's Mother and Father
Ruth Rebecca (Houchard) Patch
Jay S. Patch

FOR SALE
John Deere

Government bailout special! Runs good.
Missing steering wheel and seat.
Ideal for the person who has lost his ass
and doesn't know which way to turn.

Buds 1st & 2nd Grade Class

Bud, Buddy Patch and Joe Andrews fishing

Helen & Sister's Mabel Duffey, Irene McCormick, Elanor Firman

Earl Patch LeRoma Wariner brothers

PICTURE OF THE PAST

This 1910 picture was taken at the 50th wedding anniversary of D. B. and Lou Crottinger Patch, seated in the center of the photo. Also shown are, from left, standing: Elmo Patch, Edith Patch Beltz, Amy Patch Dunn, Daisy Patch Lowe and Dean Patch; and seated: Earl Patch, Jay Patch, Minnie Patch Streng and Irwin Patch. The picture was brought in by Opal McAlister.

Bud with Ginny and Linda Patch

Clementina Chini Torma
(Born 12/26/1915)

Clementina, known as Clem or Tina was born in Segno, Italy back in 1915. Segno is a village in North Western Italy in the region of Liguria of Vado Ligure. Both her mother, father and grandparents were natives of Segno dating back to the early 1800s. In fact, her family tree dates to the 1300s in Italy. Today Segno's countryside landscapes make it a popular venue for outdoor sports including mountain biking, cross – country running, trail and cross – country motor biking and hiking.

In 1917 her father, Richard Chini, and two of his eleven siblings, Joe and Frank yearned to find a new life in America for their family. Once they arrived in the United States they traveled west from New York and settled in a small village in eastern Ohio called Flushing (Belmont County) which is near the Ohio West Virginia border. Joe became a shoe repair man and Richard and Frank worked as coal miners. In 1920, once they had settled in to their new community Clem's father made arrangements for his family to join him here in America.

Clem, age 5, with her mother Julia and sisters Mary, Rita, and Sophie

boarded a ship (The President Wilson) heading across the Atlantic Ocean and eventually arriving safely at Ellis Island. On the way over, however, a very frightening event occurred when a passenger attempted to kidnap her sister Rita. After looking high and low Clem's mother and the boat's personnel finally located the perpetrator and returned Rita safely back to the family. What trauma! Clem tells me she remembers that event as if it happened yesterday, and of course, that was over 95years ago. As it turned out no other members of the Chini family emigrated to the United States.

Once the family was reunited in Flushing, Ohio their goal was to be able to make the most they could with what skills they had. In 1922, Clem's little brother Pio was born. Clem's father and uncle worked ten hour shifts in the coal mines six days a week in order to put food on the table. The working conditions in the mines were deplorable but tolerable. Even though this was the beginning of the roaring 1920s and the economy was steadily improving the Catholic immigrant community was still suffering. They were not owners, they were workers. Their only way to survive was the weekly paycheck they received from the coal miner's owners. Clem remembers that she and her sisters would pick up chunks of coal that had fallen off the trains while leaving the coal mines. Those chunks of coal enabled them to heat their home. In spite of the economic depression they had enough money to put food on the table and the religious faith to believe that everything would turn out okay. It did!

Clem was six years old when she attended the two- room schoolhouse until completing the eighth grade. When Clem graduated from Flushing High School in 1933, in the middle of the depression, times could not have been worse. I asked her if the family lost everything during the depression and she emphatically told me no – she said they had nothing to lose.

Soon after graduating from high school Clem and her sister Rita cleaned homes and served as nannies for families mostly in Wheeling, West Virginia. Everything seemed to be going well until December 7, 1941, the beginning of World War Two. All able-bodied young men, including her brother Pio, were drafted into the service leaving a void of factory workers to supply the goods and services needed to support the war effort. Realizing this Clem and her sister Rita moved to Mansfield, Ohio and sought employment with the Westinghouse plant where they were building airplanes for the Air Force. Believe it or not, her actual job was that of a riveter. She was one of a number of female employees known as "Rosie the Riveter". She and her fellow workers with dedication and love for the United States certainly were war heroes. We were lucky as a nation to have so many immigrants to fill the void when our men went off to war. When the war concluded in 1945 she and Rita remained at Westinghouse for the next 10 years building and assembling irons to press our clothes. From wartime to peacetime Clem's contributions as an immigrant to our country is a testimony of a true patriot. Job well done!

In 1955, at age 40, Clem was invited by one of her best girlfriends to spend some vacation time on a boat on Lake Erie. There were others on the boat that she had never met before. One of which was a fellow by the name of Eugene Torma. Clem learned that Eugene was the general superintendent of the Cleveland Convention Center and Municipal Stadium – home of the Cleveland Indians baseball team. Not only did Eugene manage the Convention Center but also handled all of the food concessions. They began dating and soon after were married. They had a wonderful life together. He was a kind, loving considerate individual. Unfortunately, one evening walking home after Mass, in a blinding snowstorm, Eugene was overcome with the sub- freezing temperature. He passed away that very evening at age 63. At age 53 Clem was now a widow.

Having worked hard her entire lifetime Clem decided that she wanted to travel and see the world. She visited Hawaii, Europe, Russia, and Ireland. She always traveled with one or two of her friends. However, when she ventured back to Segno she traveled alone. Having left Italy at five years old her memories of her old hometown were almost nonexistent. Seeing all of her relatives was a treat she will never ever

forget. Clem said to me that nothing in this world is more important than your family. Keep them close to your heart.

42 years ago, in 1976, Clem decided to move to Columbus, Ohio living on Kellner Road on the east side of Columbus. In 2006 she sold her house and moved into a retirement village and today she is in an assisted living community which fits her needs perfectly.

Clementina is a joy to behold. She came to our country as a child, grew up to support our war effort, was a loving spouse and continues to spread love with everyone she comes in contact with. She loves her nieces and nephews as if they were her own children and grandchildren. She is a testament to her religion. Even at age 102 she regularly attends Bible classes.

May she continue to lead a long and healthy life. God Bless!

The Secrets to Living Longer

The top 10 predictors of living longer

10. Clean air

9. Hypertension RX

8. Lean or Fat

7. Exercise

6. Cardiac Event

5. Flu Vaccine

4. Quit Boozing

3. Quit Smoking

2. Close Relationships

And the most important predictor is…..

1. Social Integration

According to Susan Pinker, while genetics plays 25%, our chances of living the longest will depend upon the close relationships we have as well as a high degree of social integration.

https://www.youtube.com/watch?v=ptIecdCZ3dg

About the Author

I. David Cohen

After graduating from Miami University with a Bachelor of Science degree in business in 1958 David began his career as an insurance agent and still continues this activity today. In 2002 along with co-author Keith Luscher, David wrote his first book "Get What You Want". Since that time, he has written five additional books and a play entitled "A Couple of Kids Once More" which was showcased at the Clintonville Woman's Club.

Back in 1978, as a hobby, David learned the art of Chinese cooking and throughout the last 40 years he and his wife, Rita, have entertained hundreds and hundreds of guests with their fabulous and delicious appetizers and main course dishes.

Today, his main focus is that of chronicling the lives of individuals who reached the magic age of 100 and beyond.

Epilogue

Having had the opportunity to meet and spend time with 10 seasoned citizens is something that I will never forget and will cherish for the rest of my life. In each and every case these 100-year-olds continue to possess a positive mental attitude and a zest for life. They have endured bad and sad times as well as times of extreme joy. I feel today they realize that deep down their contributions to society, community and their families has made a difference in the lives of those people they touched. These individuals are truly special.

We have chronicled over 1000 combined years of memories. Every time I hear Bob Hope Sing "Thanks for The Memory" I can only yearn for days gone by. How about you?

"Thanks for The Memory"

(Bob Hope- Helen Ross-1938)

Thanks for the memory
Of rainy afternoons, swinging Harlem tunes
Motor trips and burning lips and burning toast and prunes.
How lovely it was.
Thanks for the memory
Of candlelight and wine, castles on the Rhine,
The Parthenon, and moments on the Hudson River line.
How lovely it was.
Many's the time that we feasted
And many's the time that we fasted.
Oh well, it was swell while it lasted.
We did have fun, and no harm done.
So thanks for the memory
Of crap games on the floor, nights in Singapore.
You might have been a headache, but you never were a bore.
I thank you so much.
Thanks for the memory
Of China's funny walls, transatlantic calls.
That weekend at Niagara when we hardly saw the falls.
How lovely that was.
Thanks for the memory
Of lunch from 12 to 4, sunburn at the shore.
That pair of gay pajamas that you bought and never wore.

Say, by the way, what did happen to those pajamas?
Letters with sweet little secrets
That couldn't be put in a day wire.
Too bad it all had to go haywire.
That's life, I guess, I love your dress
Do you? Thanks for the memory
Of faults that you forgave, rainbows on a wave
And stockings in the basin when a fellow needs a shave.
I thank you so much.
Thanks for the memory
Of gardens at Versailles, and beef and kidney pie.
The night you worked and then came home with lipstick on your tie.
How lovely that was.
Thanks for the memory
Of lingerie with lace, and Pilsner by the case
And how I jumped the day you trumped my one and only ace.
How lovely that was.
We said goodbye with a highball
And I got as high as a steeple
But we were intelligent people.
No tears, no fuss, hooray for us.
Strictly entre nous, darling, how are you?
And how are all those little dreams that never did come true?
Awfully glad I met you, cheerio, tootle-oo.
Thank you, Thank you

https://www.youtube.com/watch?v=nKgUq5dziEk)

ONE FINAL THOUGHT:

Inside every 100-year-old is a younger person wondering what happened.

Made in the USA
Columbia, SC
26 June 2018